How to Build a Good Global Governance in 6 Easy Steps

Tomas Svoboda

Thank you for opening this book.

If - as I sincerely hope - you find this book interesting you are cordially invited to connect to its <u>community on Facebook</u>

This book is available for download for free in order to better spread its message. However the time and resources needed to produce the book and its followups are not free so please consider helping the effort by <u>purchasing the book or contributing by other means using this link</u>

If you have already bought and this plea is coming to you through a paid copy then please accept my big thanks.

Tomas Svoboda, the author

Table of Contents

1 ABOUT THIS BOOK..**7**
How to Read this Book.....................................7
What This Book Is About....................................7
About the Author...9
How This Book Came to Be................................10
Acknowledgments..11

2 THE CONTEXT...**13**
What We Have..13
The Things That Are Going Wrong......................15
What Should We Want?....................................22

3 PRINCIPLES, VALUES AND POWERS.........................**27**
Proportionality a.k.a. Linearity........................27
Scalability, Recursion and Transitivity...............32
The Two Real Powers.......................................35
Decision Making Based on Real Powers...............40
The Undeniable Principles................................41
Diversity...45
Tactical Considerations...................................47

4 ARCHITECTURE OF THE GLOBAL GOVERNANCE.........**55**
Obsolete Assumptions......................................55
Design Goals..56
Design Decisions...57
Institutions...63
Components of the Global Governance System......65
Rules..71
Motivations...77

5 THE 6 STEPS..**79**
Step 0: Prepare Support...................................79
Step 1: Develop Tools......................................79
Step 2: Establish Symbols................................81
Step 3: Start Small on the Bottom.....................84
Step 4: Start Small at the Top..........................86
Step 5: Close the Gap – Get Big........................87
Step 6 through ∞ : Change...............................88

6 ADDENDUM: THE ORIGINAL DOCUMENT....................**89**
The Original...89
Illustrations..90

7 INVITATION AND REQUEST.....................................**93**

How to Read this Book

This book follows a rather classical flow of thought: At first I do my best to examine the context in which Global Governance currently occurs, or fails to occur. Then I offer my own - hopefully beneficial - thoughts and finally go on to design a specific solution.

The beginning and end are of course important but frankly the essential ideas are caught in the middle. So if you would like to capture the essence first then start with chapter 3 "Principles, Values and Powers" on page 27. Two subchapters there, Proportionality a.k.a. Linearity and The Two Real Powers are the backbone of this book.

Basically what these two key subchapters have to say is that many inadequacies of current liberal democracy stem from the fact that the will of the people (voters) is transferred upwards to the governments in distorted ways. The ideal would be a directly proportional a.k.a. *linear* transfer that would carry the will of the people faithfully, right though the whole democratic decision-making process.

Another prominent idea here is that not only the number of people should be the key in the resulting voting process but also their contribution towards common efforts.

What This Book Is About

This book is an extension of a paper submitted to an international competition to design a new model of Global Governance - one example of which would be a model for a New United Nations. This book elaborates on one such model. It reconfigures the United Nations as a progressive model of governance - a Proportional Global Governance Model - that is applicable to issues both global and local. The submission itself (which was as brief as the competition rules dictated) is referenced at the end while the majority of this book describes the concept more widely and puts it into a broader context.

The bottom line is that a global decision-making mechanism can be established whose legitimacy will be derived directly from the people, thus effectively bypassing possible dysfunctionalities in their existing governments.

Coupled with sufficient moral authority and credible operating principles this can lead to a good global governance over those things that are common to all humankind.

In the submitted paper as well as in this book I concentrate specifically on the voting mechanism which is the foundation of the Governance model. Its most important properties are:

- The backbone of the (voting) model is the concept of Proportionality, which I would simplify as "striving to be directly proportional"
- Every person anywhere can vote
- Votes are weighted according to two criteria: the number of people and amount of money/effort contributed
- One may vote personally or through a representative
- The weights of the highest N voters are reduced to the value of the Nth one in order to prevent any person or group from attaining an overwhelming power.
- Continual voting serves to provide an uninterrupted timely answer to constant questions.
- Existence of "Global Identity Management System" and the "Global Transaction Verification System"

Discussion

I am sure that some will be quick to point out that this is naive, this is not how politics works. True. This is how well politics **could** work in a better world which I would love to see created.

Some of the typography used in this book:

Variable - this number or concept is likely to change in reality

References:
To make the same document usable in various environments (paper, e-book, PDF ...) I am including references and links (QR codes) directly into the text.

About the Author

I grew up in communist Czechoslovakia which gave me a chance to observe certain failed utopian dreams firsthand. The rare opportunity of spending a part of my childhood in the U.S. enabled me to compare political systems and to become infected with the American Dream and 'the Apollo optimism.' Bringing that cosmic optimism back to my country led me to several years of youthful evangelizing in the field Astronautics which became my introduction to the art of public speaking.

My father was a journalist and a writer. Through both osmosis and conscious guidance I inherited from him some of the art of writing and made it a natural habit to put my - sometimes wild - thoughts on paper. Moreover he is a devout admirer and expert on Thomas More - which gave me my baptismal name and access to a positive Utopian way of thinking.

I have proceeded to study Physics with specialization in Electronics. Most of my professional life I have spent on designing electronic and ICT systems and managing projects in that area. Therefore my prevailing frame of mind is "how to design it so that it works".

I also have some limited practical experience in politics which leaves me wondering how could we ever have ended with systems so senseless.

How This Book Came to Be

It is so very presumptuous to think that a simple engineering manager with limited political experience from a medium city in a small country could contribute to global thinking about how to solve the largest challenges of mankind. However the thoughts and trends emerged as so obvious and needing to be stated. So much for my public apology for thinking big.

I started writing down some of my thoughts in 2016. The year was significant in two ways: Firstly I had undergone a surgery and had a lot of free time in the hospital and afterwards. Secondly it was the 500th anniversary of the publication of the classic Utopia by Thomas More and I had a strong urge to do something about the occasion. I did write a few chapters but nothing really definitive. Then real life prevailed and my Utopian writing was sidetracked.

The deciding impulse that propelled me towards writing this book came from the "Global Challenges Foundation"'s https://www.globalchallenges.org/ in 2017 announcement of a competition to design a new Global Governance Model – which had been the topic of many of my thoughts. The competition with a fixed deadline gave me what I needed to advance in my writing and made me complete a few coherent chapters which form the basis of this book. The challenge also helped me to focus on just one topic of the wide Utopian horizon. In this book I am making the view wider again and reminding myself how difficult it is to get all the thoughts organized without the focusing theme.

Originally the title of the book was *"How to Set Up a Good Global Government ..."* which reflected my older thinking along the lines of extrapolating traditional government structures to a global scope. However under the influence of the competition I have gradually modified both my thinking and the title.

One of my continuing priorities is keeping things simple in the interest of their clarity and transparency. For this reason I will do my best to keep this book short and specific. This will especially mean concentrating on the topic of Global Governance and not dwelling too long on general reasoning.

2019-03-27 :
Beginning with version 7.0 I am introducing a major change in terminology: I will now be using the key term **"Proportional"** instead of "~~Linear~~" because the latter has led to some major misunderstanding.

Acknowledgments

The title has been inspired by „*The Millennial Project: Colonizing the Galaxy in Eight Easy Steps*" an excellent book by Marshall T. Savage.

Big thanks to my friends, especially Heather MacGillivray, Mardi Shakti, Alexandra Alvarová and others whose feedback has been extremely helpful in preparing the entry for the competition and this book.

The elegant cover was created by Namona Design
www.namona-design.com

What We Have

In the spirit of project management I like to begin any effort by looking at the current situation and characterizing what is important about it and what we want to change. This is the purpose of this chapter.

However I often tend to jump ahead of myself to conclusions and solutions (*and I have jumped ahead, here, to the issues of Global Governance*) so please forgive me for having done that in this chapter ... but I think the result, of my injecting my thoughts and conclusions as I go, is that this section is not the boring inventory it might otherwise have been been.

The Good Things That We Already Have

We have unprecedented abilities and resources in many areas:

- For the first time in history we have the means to feed every human
- Science and technology provide us with endless possibilities to affecting the surrounding natural environment
  - Including new means of organizing human society
- New communication abilities

We have powers available now that would have been considered impossible not long ago. In many fields explosive improvement is taking place. A fascinating account is available from the World Economic Forum. However all the good developments are not enough as huge challenges also appear.

Currently about a half of global population have some kind of connectivity at least once in a while. However the unconnected population is to be reduced soon through direct satellite connectivity which is aimed specifically at underdeveloped regions of Africa and elsewhere.

Universal access to information is a precondition to the whole governance model contained in this book.

National governments are failing in a global world

There is a prevailing feeling that the national governments are failing at their task of representing their people and at executing the collective will of the people in the interest of their common good. To some extent these feelings are malevolently amplified or even started by destructive forces (e.g. the disinformation campaigns attributed to various rogue states and evil organizations) but they do have some real core.

This massive failure may be the manifestation of deficiencies in the existing models of governance. Moreover when it comes to really global phenomena the national states have their hands tied by each other's sovereignty.

Beware of Extrapolation

It is too easy to propose governance on the global level by extrapolating (= enlarging without a deeper change) mechanism that function (and fail) on the smaller scale. *E.g. to propose a global parliament of elected representatives consisting of 2 chambers.*

As we would not want to bring the same dysfunctions from local to the global level we must think carefully when designing a model of global governance

Failure of Technology?

Another widespread point of view sees it that technology and "hard sciences" have failed in providing for humankind the expected 'wonderful future'. I strongly disagree: A failure of technology is a car that does not start or a bomb that explodes prematurely or a building that collapses. Providing a bright future is not a function of technology; if that was an expectation it was unfounded.

Yes, technology can do a lot to help make the future better but shaping the future is a task of politics, societal functions, justice, governance, religion etc. etc. These all together are responsible for the better future. Science and Technology are just 'tools.'

One might rephrase the complaint about technology in another way: *"With such immense advances that we see in technology and science why do we not experience similar advances in the betterment of human society?"* I believe that is the correct question. Technology and sciences – used as tools - have brought about a lot of impressive progress not only in the excellent functioning of various mechanisms but also in optimizing the organization within different types of systems (including optimizing the human "factor") for better performance - and these methods could be used very directly for the common good - specifically to create a better governance system.

However attempts to apply some of the technological and scientific principles to governing the society tend to be quickly dismissed as "technocracy" ("κράτος" "kratos" - power) as if technology itself was trying to take away the power from someone not willing to release that power. *(Could that even be the case?)*

One might even argue that technology *has not been allowed* to improve the world as much as it could have done. It seems that we as a society should learn how to better utilize technology to make more use of its potential blessings. In this book I would like to give some help in that direction.

As a poignant example look at the current (2019/2020) wave of wildfires in Australia where the national government totally ignored the possibility of satellite fire detection and use of water bombers for mitigation. They even refused international offers of help using these airplanes.

The word "seems" is crucial. We in the West live in the best times ever experienced by humankind (according to various measurable indexes) but still we often feel misrepresented and mismanaged.

One way of looking at this situation is that there is no global politics yet though many other industries and facets of life have been strongly globalized.

Complexity

One of the perceived problems of the current society is its overwhelming complexity which induces the perception of non-transparency and inability to influence the common things.

Global capitalism seems to be failing

Even though according to many indicators we are living in the best of times there exists a prevailing notion that the system is doing a bad job at making people happy. This notion is closely tied to the perceived failure of politics – so closely that it may well be impossible to reform/create a global governance without reforming the global economy as well.

Capitalism has become global and found ways to easily transgress national borders and use them to its own advantage (beginning with the well known havens for tax evasion). Therefore efforts to reform capitalism will also have to be coordinated on a global level.

We are approaching the time when (as the founding theoreticians of communism have predicted) the technological power of manufacturing will be able to produce an abundance of (almost) anything for everyone. The big question is how to make this abundance serve to everyone's happiness.

Some of the economic principles of Capitalism requiring revision
may be:

- Natural resources are free to be taken by liberal capitalism
- People are free to be used by employers and to be disposed of thereafter
- Money is the omnipotent numeraire/quantifier that defines almost everything else
- There is no upper limit on the accumulation of wealth while there is a sharp existential lower limit (*having* zero money)

The solutions may include

- Making the commercial usage of natural resources expensive

- Applying some form of public control over companies, especially the large ones with global influence

- Implementing global rules for the movement of money across national borders

- Making money less important for people's living (unimaginable when looking through the periscope of liberal capitalism).

  → *The previous bullet is a huge topic in itself as both big ideologies of the 20th century – liberal capitalism and communism lead us into the same trap – a belief that all is about possession and its (re)distribution. And they further strengthened this illusion using the image of right-left political spectrum.*

Here I got ahead of myself in not just enumerating the deficiencies of the current status quo but also proposing solutions. Well it just did not fit anywhere else in this book :-)

Lack of Systems Approach

This may be an important obstacle that is preventing us from creating something new: Those responsible for public decision-making are often unaware of rational methods of management or refuse them outright.

I have seen politicians who refuse a rule that would be formulated by a simple mathematical equation for some irrational fear of things "too complicated". While in reality all other options of formulating the rule in imprecise human language tend to lead to more ambiguity and complexity.

This unwillingness to act in rational ways may be the single most important barrier on the way toward a better future.

The Things That We Lack

Common Arbiter

Many have already written that violent conflicts will inevitably arise whenever the conflicting parties have no common authority above them that could resolve their differences and quarrels. *(e.g. Emery Reeves, The Anatomy of Peace)*

Deep in history it was left to God's proxies – the Churches – to fulfill this role. It did work to some extent but after Humanism placed the humans above God this option lost its ground. However this 'common authority' approach does tend to return in the form of moral authority which may be very beneficial.

There are some current attempts to establish supranational authorities based on voluntary consent between states e.g. the United Nations, European Union or the International Court of Human Rights. These do have some limited success but remain far from solving all relevant issues.

Currently conflicts do start and the price of resolving international and inter-state conflicts in money and human suffering is escalating beyond any reasonable limits.

It is often objected "Who will watch the watchers?", "Who will tame the tamers?" in the sense that a single super-ordinate authority might turn up bad. Yes this is a true risk. And it seems self-evident, that any such authority will appear bad to some people. However even if such a super-authority conducted itself really badly it still could provide ANY arbitrations which would be better than no arbitration and never ending conflicts among "sovereign" states.

To quote the recent classic: Yes, there are substantial risks but, on the other hand, <u>without a 'world government' technology will destroy us, says Stephen Hawking</u>

Verification

A lesser function similar to common arbitrage is the objective verification of local governments' information and claims.

Independent oversight

National governments have a difficult task setting up really independent authorities for regulation, justice and oversight. Overcoming this problem is attempted by lifelong mandates and various certitudes that make the persons less dependent on the temporary influences from their government. However there always remains some level of dependence on the government or parliament which issue the nominations.

Delegating a part of the nominating process upward to the global structures could contribute toward the real independence of the local authorities. That is true under the condition that the global governance is not deeply engaged in the problems of regional governances and thus is really independent.

One might argue that this would only move the problem upward to the global level. True. This might lead us to believe that most of the independent authority work should be done on the regional level to reduce the risk of global independent authorities being appointed with no one above them to guarantee their independence.

Global Authority to Respond to Common Challenges

It is self-evident that reaching agreements among states about cooperating toward common goals, is extremely difficult because the benefit goes to all but the expenses have to be shared in an arbitrary way. In these situations it is usual for states to try to minimize their contribution and let others do the paying.

The common global goals include: Ecology, Usage of natural resources, Disaster response, Human rights, Truthful reporting, Genetic degradation, Planetary defense...

For solving these challenges we clearly lack a common authority.

As it seems from various scenarios foreseen in literature and elsewhere: Response to a common global challenge by multiple "sovereign" states divided by their perceived differing interests and varying access to information may become very counterproductive, even worse that the original challenge itself *(for just one flashing example see the TV drama Salvation of 2017)*. Such a perspective gives a powerful reason for needing a strong global decision-making authority.

After spelling out the current status the next logical step is to try to outline what we would like the status to be and how different it should be from the current one.

Do we really need a global governance or government? In a situation when powerful voices speak out against 'global' wanting to, instead, direct us back towards 'local,' what should we do? Do we need to create something that might eventually fail on a global scale? Are there any compelling tasks or problems that call for a global power to solve them?

In this chapter let us establish the reasons why a common global decision-making power is absolutely positively necessary.

The Big Question: The Main Goal

What is the ultimate goal we would as humankind want to achieve? The answer is a difficult one to find and multi-faceted in the goals it is comprised of.

One obvious goal is survival; the survival of humankind as a whole species and prevention of mass deaths and suffering in avoidable disasters. Another one is to preserve civilization as we know it and avoid a painful restart.

The goal might very well include freedom, security or lack of stress for human beings or the fulfillment of their basic needs.

Maybe the best formulation of the big goal comes from the Pope John Paul II: *"To build a world where it would be easier to be good."*

Any better ideas?

It has often been said that those who try to create a heaven on Earth usually end up creating hell. In real history this happens mostly through setting unrealistic goals and through poor execution that creates more problems than it solves (Communism, Nazism etc.).

However there is strong evidence that if an ideal environment is created which fulfills all the needs of its inhabitants and makes them free of labor, struggle and conflict they will still be less than happy. *(Calhoun rats)* This is probably because we - animals - are not wired for stressless life but rather for a life of struggling, striving and limitations.

Perhaps we can see some of the Calhoun effect in the rich countries of Europe where despite of all the material well-being and measurable improvement there seems to be less happiness than expected.

What is Best

It seems that the optimal environment for human beings is such where an individual needs to strive toward achieving their existential needs like procreation, social status, material wealth etc. The barriers to achieving these goals should be such that most people succeed during their lifetimes and only a small number fail.

If everyone did succeed it would mean that it was too easy - therefore we do need the small failing minority both for calibration of the system and as a motivational example for all. How the failure should manifest itself is another question and it does not have to be as hard as in history - like hunger and death. Reasonable social nets can make the failure reasonably soft while still considerably uncomfortable.

Then there is the other end of the Gaussian curve - those who succeed in a spectacular way. Again it would be wise for these to be a small minority for the same reasons like with the failures.

Boundaries and Formation

Especially in one's youthful formation years it is essential to have adequate boundaries and challenges set up to enable them to overcome difficulties and establish their place in the human society. Apart from the social systems this has to do with education and other formative systems e.g. a compulsory (military or civil) service.

Particular Goals

After reaching a certainty that a global power is necessary for solving some acute problems it would be beneficial to look at a wider perspective of what good we might expect from a global coordinating power. So, before beginning to seriously think about any kind of world governance we should be clear about what we want from it and how it would benefit the people – and which people specifically.

There are some general wishful-thinking trends that offer themselves to solving problems on a global scale, which are, among others:

- Reconciliation between the Local and Global
- Reconciliation between the Rich, the Able and the Rest
- Reconciliation between the rich and poor regions
- Finding a balance between the strong inflow of information and weak ability to influence
- Finding a balance between the benign power of technology and enslavement by that technology
- Empowerment of everyone
- Simplifying the unmanageable complexity of the world

At this point I feel a strong temptation to try solving all the world's problems at once which is unrealistic. However it is reasonable to believe that if we set up good foundations – get the governance right – some of the other solutions will tend to fall into place and some of the problems will take care of themselves. So let us focus on the governance.

A very good and more specific compilation of desirable Humankind's goals comes from the United Nations as "The 17 sustainable development goals (SDGs) to transform our world"

We have seen many proposals to extrapolate the structures of existing liberal democracies toward the global level with a Global Parliament, Global Government, Global Justice etc. etc. all elected and nominated like they usually are in nation-states. This would probably create huge managerial structures with all the problems (amplified) of top-heavy national and federal governments.

The question is how much direct executive power do we want to delegate to the global level. I believe that – in order to avoid a huge global bureaucracy – it should be as little as possible. The global executive branches do seem necessary for some specialized global tasks which do not divide across regions e.g. Planetary Defense, Climate, ...

However for most fields it would seem that a global coordinating body should work well with executive bodies on regional levels. E.g. for Disaster Response it would be nice to have a global body to coordinate the pooling and sharing of resources but effective actions would best be undertaken by regional units.

I believe it would be good to have a constant tension between the Global and the Local regarding their competencies. As it is impossible to define upfront which issues should be decided on global level and which are better handled on local level it will be best to facilitate an ongoing process that will be able to make these decisions effectively.

The previous views lead me to believe that the world needs Governance rather than a global government or global management as per the excellent UNESCO definition.

> *„Before you start worrying about the mechanics*
> *be sure you understand the thermodynamics"*
> a rocket scientist's proverb

In this chapter (before we go on to design the new system of Global Governance) I would like to review some of the basic principles that we should be aware of and work with.

The human society is a system as defined in various sciences like cybernetics. And it behaves like one – whether we like it or not. Meaning that it obeys some objective laws even though the image may be too cluttered to recognize that behavior easily.

It is about measurement: If it can be measured it can be explored and perhaps controlled better than something immeasurable.

Proportionality a.k.a. Linearity

Definition:

Let us begin by clarifying the word: **PROPORTIONAL**
In this book let us understand this concept as "directly proportional" - as a situation where the output of a process or a system matches its input in the most exact or proportional way.

Throughout the proposed model I try to apply the principle of Proportionality which means that things should behave similarly in various contexts – namely in local and global governance. E.g. it should work in a very similar way whether a person is voting about a local decision or about something as global as a 'carbon tax'. Thus let us try to show that local and global governance can work on the same principles and coexist fruitfully with each other.

In this section let me try to explain that in order to create a smoothly running system it is often advantageous if information in that system travels in a proportional fashion meaning that it is transmitted through the structure of the system without unnecessary distortion.

Our main point is that throughout history many non-proportional transformations had to be introduced into public decision-making systems to compensate for the then-current inability to process all necessary information in real time. However nowadays it is realistic to process all imaginable quantities of information in short time therefore allowing for example all the people on Earth to vote on an issue within minutes.

Moreover: Throughout history it took a long time and indirect interpretation for decisions from the top to reach people at the bottom. Nowadays news travels very fast and all people get swift feedback about decisions that affect their lives. This increases their frustration about their inability to influence those decisions. Having information travel directly in both directions opens the potential for an entirely new participatory way of governance.

What is Proportionality

The term "proportionality" is borrowed from Systems Theory which is very relevant to systems of governance in human society. Though many aspects of human society are not measurable we try to create abstractions using measurable values thus increasing our understanding and command over these.

In theory a function is considered proportional *(a.k.a. linear)* if its output is directly commensurate to its input. Like pressing the gas pedal in a car results in (approximately) proportional speed of movement of the car. However when we reach some speed we cannot go much faster – this is one example of non-proportionality. Another example of non-proportional behavior is when we run out of fuel or the car crashes and suddenly the movement of the car is not proportional to our stepping on the pedal.

It is clear that while in proportional mode (the medium range of speed) the car is easily controllable and predictable. It just works fine. However when the car gets out of the proportional mode we may find it difficult or impossible to control its movement and destiny.

It is the same way with many other systems in both technology and society. Proportional systems are easy to predict and control while non-proportional systems tend to give us a hard time. It is important to realize that our society, local and global is a very very non-proportional system of systems. Making the decision-making processes in the society more proportional is one way toward regaining some more control of our common destiny – and taking that control away from those who try to abuse the many discrepancies (a.k.a. non-proportionalities) in our existing governance models.

Proportionality in time

A system proportional in time would be one that does not change its behavior. Meaning that it reacts to your input in the same way / producing the same output regardless of when you apply the input.

This can be compared to an overnight vending machine – whenever you insert a payment you receive a soft drink or whatever. That is behavior proportional in time. However in a brick store which closes at night the behavior is strongly non-proportional – its output is zero all night.

In current election systems there is a sharp temporal non-proportionality: One day (on election day) your opinion matters and the next day it does not for the following four or five years. This contributes greatly to perceived contrasts between behavior in election campaigns and after election.

I would like to see a system of governance that is proportional in time – meaning that whenever I – the voter – express my small opinion it will always have the same small but measurable impact.

This is the ideal but there are many necessary non-proportionalities. For example there has to be some moment when a decision (e.g. to start building a bridge) is final and partial opinions do not matter any more. However there are cases where time-proportional behavior is possible and beneficial.

Proportionality in weight of vote

In current parliamentary systems the weight of individual votes is changed greatly due to various counting models – in the extreme case the opinion of a minority is ignored if it is smaller that the "Election threshold" of 5% or similar. In a proportional system each voter should have a guarantee that their small vote is included in the final counting even if it is just one billionth of the total. It is not just to give everyone a fair chance but even more to prevent various distortions (a.k.a. non-proportionalities) associated with artificial limits and boundaries inserted into the process.

Delegation and (non)proportionality

After being elected to office a person is made relatively independent on the opinions of the electorate. There is some remaining dependence through parliamentary negotiations, impeachment etc. which is highly nonproportional and is activated only under some conditions.
This independence leads to a difference between actions of the elect and their previous promises (presumably equal to the will of the voters).
In a proportional model the voter would be free to rethink their election at any time so the elected person would be in a constant need of keeping their voters satisfied (However there is a thin

line between this direct influence and populism which should not be crossed.)

One very important source of non-proportionality is the necessity in current democracies to transform the large number of votes into small integer number of elected persons. This happens either through a majority system or some form which may even call itself proportional. All of these systems contain inheren disproportions due to the simple fact that there is no way of faithfully converting large numbers into small integers. Often these disproportions are so huge that they may even reverse the voters' will completely as it has in 2019 general election in the UK: The majority of people have voted for parties opposed to Brexit but the majority system has distributed the seats in the parliament in a way that strongly favors Brexit.

(see https://www.theneweuropean.co.uk/top-stories/more-than-52-of-the-general-election-vote-went-to-pro-remain-parties-1-6424196 *)*

One huge non-proportionality – so overwhelming that it would probably even fall outside of the category – is the fact that we elect the people to become the top managers of our world (elected officials) not on the basis of their management competencies but based on their acting abilities and power of influence. As a result the elections in western democracies have degraded from a competition of programs to a fight for personal and collective power.

Necessary non-proportionalities

Just like our ancestors were forced to include many non-proportional components in their democratic processes we also see such a need though on a smaller scale. Some of the important cases are:

An efficient decision-making system has to include some inertia so that it does not react too hastily or impetuously to its inputs. Too quick a reaction can lead to instability of a system (through over-reacting e.g. taking action in the correct direction which overshoots the intended target and moves the system too far from its optimal state) which itself leads away from proportional behavior. Therefore "dampers" need to be included in the system that would absorb or slow down some effects of quickly changing inputs.

Protection of minorities versus majorities/monopolies

In a proportional system one influence can attain more power than others and effectively take over. It is wise to include measures against such possible behavior.

Scalability

Based on technological and organizational estimates the presented Governance Model (if implemented well) can scale up to at least 100 billion participants (in U.S. English = 10 to the 11th power).

In the downward direction the model can scale down to approximately 100 participants so it can be used even in very small public subspaces.

Recursion

Recursion in computer science means that inside some object another object of similar properties can exist. The trick is that both the inner and outer object behave similarly and can be worked with in similar ways.

A real-world example could be a branch on a tree. There is a big branch from which a smaller branch grows. Both can be described in similar terms e.g. length, mass, number of leaves etc. On any of these one could perform the same operations e.g. cut off, shorten, paint, disinfect, etc.

Inside a system of governance (like the global one we are imagining) there can be another (recursive) one governed in the same or similar way. Inside the Global Council there can be an American or Asian (etc.) council operating on the same principles and sharing some of its members/voters.

Departmental Recursion

A Global Governance system will naturally deal not only with general issues but also with specialized ones. For example we may see a global discussion whether to prioritize a mission to

Mars or a lunar base. Only a minority of humankind will have something to say about it. For that globe-spanning minority however this may be an important, almost existential, question.

For such specialized decisions it would be natural to sub-organize the Global Governance model into multiple specialized "councils". It would seem practical to somehow enforce the separation of voters across these groups e.g. by allowing each voter to vote only in one specialty group or similarly.

- This is beyond the scope of this book and should be elaborated to more detail in the future.

Transitivity

Proportional systems are transitive in the sense that through whatever number and order of proportional transformations the input/signal passes the result still stays proportional to the original input. (*Mathematicians please forgive me.*)

In politics this might mean less importance for arbitrary organizational units. E.g. we have strong separatist movement let's say in Catalunya who strongly believe it would be better to make their decisions outside of the Spanish decision-making system because their will does not pass well through the Spanish system. (And much violence stems from such non-proportionalities/non-transitivities in our civilization). Now let us imagine that both Catalunya and the rest of Spain would be a part of the same proportional/transitive voting/decision-making system: They would be voting about an issue in their region like perhaps the appointment of a police chief and his budget – the result would be the same whether they are voting within a Catalunyan or Spanish state. Then suddenly the votes of Catalunyan voters would apply in the system like those of everyone else and separatism would not really matter because the people would be making their decisions in a transparent transitive mode anyway.

There are things that need to be decided together on a global level.

Among the issues that should remain to be decided on a regional level there are such that should be defined globally and parameterized on a regional level.

For example there could be a global definition of what is a handgun (defined perhaps by caliber, length, number of shots in the magazine, mode of carrying etc.) with certain global limitations. The regions would be free to use this definition to assert what guns may be owned and carried on their territory and whether a gun may or must not be carried concealed. Not that every state would have come up with its own legal definition (causing overlaps at borders). Also for regions that do not impose their parameters there would be a default global value.

Another example: A global rule could be that all new buildings must be prepared to handle an H high layer of snow where the H can vary from 0 to infinity. Kenya would probably set H=0 while Finland would opt for a higher layer.

Power 1: The People

It has been an axiom in most democracies that all people are equal and therefore must have the same decision-making influence. That is a solid principle which should be upheld. Every human being is something real and well defined – there are no legal tricks for splitting a human being into two or merging them into one. That gives a solid base for construction of predictable decision-making systems.

It used to be impossible to interact in real time with millions of decision-makers so their power was exercised through representation and imperfect voting systems. This limitation is no longer necessary – thanks to advances in computing power we now are able to interact with billions of people and keep account of their inputs in real time and in fail-safe accountable manner.

Counting People

It is self-evident that in order to determine the voting power of a group (e.g. a nation) it is necessary to account for all its members. In ancient cultures this was seen as blasphemy as only God was supposed to have an overview of all his subjects. However nowadays there may the advantage that if people are accounted for they might not get lost as easily (as they sometimes do in some dictatorships) and their country would have to accept some level of responsibility for them.

However many see a downside: Census and registering of citizens are often feared as enablers of oppression. Many wish for an idealized society of the past with no IDs and no governmental oversight as to the citizens' identities. In this view the liberty of the individual is preserved when no information about them exists. I am afraid that this is not realistic any more.

Information about individuals do exist and are widely used and we as a society are only learning how to tame those usages.

There is one peculiar requirement: One's identity must be maintained constant throughout that person's life. We in the western countries take this for granted but I have learned that this may not be the case in some cultures.

I do believe that registering people is unavoidable. In order for a person to participate in common things there has to be some record to document their legitimacy.

It is crucial however to be very strong and smart about preventing any possible abuse of such centrally maintained information. I can well imagine that in a future society the abuse of central data might become one of the most severe crimes analogous to a high treason.

Power 2: Money

We have long surpassed the Pareto principle of 80/20 where 20% people should hold 80% of resources. Now we are somewhere around or above 95/5 which (efficiency and justice aside) means that there is huge – maybe absolute – power in the hands of corporations and individuals.

It is often argued that money (especially in its current virtual forms) is a fictive concept. However for the purpose of these thoughts we would like to speak of „money" as something reasonably real that represents a measure of people's (and organizations') effort or contribution to a common goal. In this sense "money" is another real power that makes the difference between success and failure.

It seems natural to assume that whoever contributes more „money" to an effort should also have a proportional influence on decisions about that effort. Unlike in current tax systems (simplification) where most money is taken from the successful while the spending is decided by "all".

From the perspective of the starting Global Governance: The contributions counted toward voting weight can be voluntary contributions at the beginning and possibly could later morph into some form of global tax system – the proposed and idealized "Carbon tax" is an excellent opportunity.

To put this into current context let us recall - president Trump's speech at the U.N. where he complained about the U.S. paying most of the United Nations' expenses while exercising very little influence. The present Proportional Governance model would be a step toward repairing that discrepancy.

I do not endorse Trump in most of what he stands for and understand how counterproductive it might be even to just quote him but this seems like a valid example.

Clarification

The idea of granting voting powers based ofn financial contributions attracts a lot of opposition. The first argument against it is that this would give even more power to the plutocrats who are enjoying too much influence even now. It is not meant so. It is meant for the rich people's influence to come out of the shadows *(of lobbying and corruption)* and become legal and regulated. One might recall a quote attributed to Hegel: „*Freedom is a recognized necessity*" in the sense that money is going to translate into power anyway so why not subordinate its influence to rules.

While the resulting (possibly extreme) voting power of the very rich attracts the first level of attention the proposal is meant specifically to favor the middle class – the masses of people who have done their share for the society and achieved something meaningful – at least in financial terms. To amplify this I would tend to favor some form of limitation at the upper end.

> *In other words: This is not to empower the big money. This is to empower the middle-class money and people.*

One important aspect of this proposition is that it takes into account only legal money that has gone through the correct process of accounting and taxation. The shady money from criminal activities and from doubtful foreign sources (which poses the biggest danger to the current democracy) would be left out.

I would like to point out that the proposed voting power is derived solely from contributions (taxes or other) not from accumulated wealth.

In implementation the voting power could be derived not only from financial contributions but perhaps from other forms of contribution. However a very careful reasoning would be needed not to break the proportionality principle.

And last not least I would propose contribution-based voting only as one of multiple criteria, never a single key to voting power.

Gratitude

Once a person's contribution is measured and recorded the global society in this proposal shows its gratitude by allowing that person a measure of decision-making power. However that does not have to be the only instance of gratitude for their contribution. An obvious one would be an increase in that person's social/financial security - through pension/health/insurance accounts. Thus maybe we could be bypassing one huge motivation for senseless accumulation of wealth by individuals which is to secure one's future way of life. It would be a wonderful world where paying one's taxes would be an efficient way of investing toward one's life at old age.

I can think of many other perks that could be offered to successful contributors. For example I would not mind if the greatest taxpayer in my city was allowed to drive with a police siren or speak on TV on New Year etc. etc.

In this point the design of the Global Governance closely interfaces with the design of the Global Economy.

Other Powers

Apart from the 2 previous powers one could identify further important global powers. However to keep the complexity low let us rather limit our thoughts to the 2 preceding powers.
One could certainly remember nations – one nation one vote – as a specific body of power. However nations constantly split or

unite and vary in size and in intensity of their members' identification. So nations would be something very difficult to measure and agree on.

A similarly ambiguous status would apply to the category "political power" - an immeasurable mixture of past credit, military capability and institutional relationships - on which the United Nations were based. If it cannot be measured it cannot be later used to adjust the system and this is what keeps the U.N. anchored to the past and unable to shape the future.

Decision Making Based on Real Powers

When decisions are based on real measurable (accountable) powers and influences they tend to survive in the real world even if the world changes to some extent. Whenever decisions are based on superficial rules or fictive concepts they tend to be overrun by real powers and bypassed organically by any mechanism available.

To illustrate this notion let us imagine the crossing of a wide long distance road and a small country road. It is natural and "real" for the traffic on the large road to have priority. Should we set up a traffic sign giving priority to the small road we would probably see accidents caused by difference between the usual perception of reality and the "unreal" traffic signs.

This is the current situation where laws and important decisions are made by all the people in a democratic process – which is sometimes less „real" than the anonymous power of big money. Money is so powerful that it exerts its influence into politics – which is considered wrong a.k.a. corrupt. This is the direct result of pretending that the power of the democratic process is real and uncontested.

In a balanced decision making process that would reflect the real powers the voting power must be weighed by both the people

(every human has the same weight) and by money/contribution.
To illustrate this principle we can imagine a parliament where
one chamber is elected one-person-one-vote while the votes for
the second chamber are commensurate to tax contributions
from individual voters.

The Undeniable Principles

In this chapter I would like to outline some very basic principles which should underlay any moral system of governance. Please excuse if I am getting too general or corny here - I do believe that the foundations of any good endeavor have to be solid and sound moral principles belong to this solidness.

Truth Exists

The tension between truth and lie often goes hand in hand with the struggle between good and evil. And there are good reasons to connect truth with a common good. Among all reasons there is transparency: If we openly share one truth we can more easily find a common ground for agreeing on common decisions.

In the so-called post-truth situation it is essential to realize that facts do exist and so does objective truth on many issues. On these facts, not on hypotheses must be based any meaningful effort for betterment of the society.

Actually it is the tactics of destructive powers to relativize all truth and thus enforce chaos in the society. For supporting a cohesive society it is important to counteract these by promoting truth and making it clearly visible.

It can be argued that societies can exist who do not rely on objective truth as much as our Judeo-Christian culture. However it is this type of culture that brought the technological civilization to its current level and I strongly believe that strict reliance on objective truth is the only way forward.

Networks of Trust

There have always been invisible and spontaneous networks of people that trusted each other and relayed that trust via their connections.

In the digital world where it is more difficult to assess someone's trustworthiness there have been numerous attempts to establish formalized "Networks of Trust". Some of these attempts have been made by the classics of benevolent encryption Zimmerman and Shuttleworth to ensure the public an access to reliable digital signatures. The methodology is either

- that all trust is derived from one ultimately trusted person (typically the founder) who then relays that trust through a hierarchy of proven contacts

- or between any two persons the level of trust is derived from the "distance" of connections between them.

Taken to a higher level such techniques could help ensure the validity of shared information – a core component of informed public decision/making.

I would even go as far as to say that sharing of trust is critically needed in today's digital society: We are very good at online sharing of information, perceptions, resources, connexxions etc. However trust still remains to be effectively shared.

Human Rights

It has taken millions of deaths in the 20th century and immeasurable suffering to come up with a reasonable definition of what one human must never deny another (basic human rights). This definition must be the undoubted axiom of any healthy future global efforts.

As important as the Human Rights are one should never neglect their inseparable complement – the undefined Human Duties. One simplistic way of looking at this is that everyone has the duty of granting basic human rights to everyone else. However it seems natural that our human duties should go beyond these basics.

44

Code of Behavior

It might seem out of place to discuss this broad general concept in the context of a governance system. However i do believe that morality is a cornerstone of any governance so i am including this one.

We Do Not Kill

The most basic code of collective behavior is: No human may be killed in the course of establishing a common good. If a single human should be killed under the guise of common good that would be a reason to quickly dismantle the mechanisms that led to the death. Not killing people certainly is not sufficient to define good behavior but it is the lowest limit that must never be violated. We have seen so many utopian efforts that shifted toward murderous tyrannies that it almost seems like a litmus test of an effort going wrong. That must be observed and avoided at all cost.

Of course this relates directly to the issue of capital punishment. The right to live is probably the most important of human rights (defined above) which inevitably leads to a ban on capital punishment. For me as a European this seems self-evident and it is difficult for me to understand that some countries and people would fight hard to maintain the death penalty. Nevertheless their opinion must be respected.

Trustworthiness

Personal integrity of those seeking public office is paramount.

Those who seek to have roles in decision-making should expect to sacrifice something in return. The sacrifice certainly includes some invasion of privacy because we have grown to expect some transparency and insight into the lives of our leaders.

Additionally it would be best for the leaders to sacrifice even more: It would be very healthy for someone in a public office to give up their option to accrue wealth (temporarily or for the rest of their lives) and depend entirely on pay or pension coming from that office. It would certainly eliminate much of suspicions of corruption we face today – and entrusting one's (financial) security to a trustworthy government would also liberate them from the omnipresent capitalist drive to secure their own future.

Such an arrangement would be similar to the constitutions ruling monastic orders which also required strict dedication and exclusive dependence from their members. The monastic orders went even further: They disallowed their members any (marital or sexual) relationships that could get in the way of their mission. In the not so distant past such restrictions were common for many public services, even lowly such as schoolteachers and soldiers. Is this too much to ask of our leaders and administrators?

Diversity

Diversity is a value in its own right because it enables the birth and growth of minority trends – which may later evolve into important ones. Therefore supporting diversity of opinions and goals should be a reasonable thing to do.

However currently we see an overdoing of diversity often ridiculed as "Political Correctness" where every minority trend – however silly or counter-cultural - claims the right to equality, to being respected and treated as important. This is not a productive way – a trend has to earn its place among the respected ones by working its way up from peripheral to recognized.

Diversity Against Societal Addictions

We as a society are growing more and more addicted to a variety of goods including such as running water, processed food, eyeglasses, intensive medical care. While each of these is a good in its own right we are growing less and less capable of surviving without them. Therefore it is extremely desirable to have minority movements that tend to live without some of these addictions.

On a smaller scale it is useful to have communities like Boy Scouts that at least teach and preserve the arts of living without some goods of civilization.

Global Totality?

This dystopian possibility would be an opposite of healthy diversity: A totality can well be defined as a system that does not allow its subjects to escape from that system. In current regional totalities the ultimate escape is immigration to another region.

However when certain decisions and/or structures become valid on a global level the globality may well limit people's ability to escape from them. An example of this unlucky trend might be the current financial system which tends to become the single unavoidable norm for people in the west/north and tries to embrace the developing countries as well.

Creating a global totality certainly is a danger that must be avoided very carefully.

A well thought out non-totalitarian global system should include options for people to escape or avoid the complexities or decisions of that system. How exactly that should be done I cannot say yet, I just know that it should be so. One example of such an escape option appears in sci-fi literature as the "Island of Oblivion" in Yefremov's classic the "Andromeda Nebula" (the book, not the movie). In that scenario people unable to cope with the rules of the utopian society would go to an unregulated environment on a remote tropical island.

Maybe (please don't catch me on this one) one could even think of something like a voluntary prison system where one could have their needs taken care of in exchange for some limitation of their liberty for as long as they want to stay out of the complex outside world. (*One peculiarity that leads me to this thought is African refugees trying to commit crimes in Scandinavia and be jailed because living in a Scandinavian prison is much much better than living free in some countries.*)

In the previous text we have looked at the most important strategic "backbone" principles. Let us now deal with some of the more practical lower level - though also important – principles which would tell us **how** to achieve what we want.

Concentration of Power

In most democratic (and dictatorial even more) management systems we see positive feedback effects that tend to give more power to the already powerful leading to increasing concentration of power in one or more nuclei.

I am writing this shortly after parliamentary elections in 2017 in the Czech Republic when we are widely criticizing our system of vote counting which excessively favors the big parties to the extent that the biggest party needed 18700 votes to achieve one mandate while the smallest one had to collect 52300 – not even counting the parties that did not pass the minimum clause at all.

Even without such explicit injustices there are natural effects that help concentrate power: One who has power attracts attention and therefore is in advantageous position to capture opportunities for attaining more power. *"Money attracts money, Positions attract positions"*.

In a truly representative, proportional, system it would be good to weaken such effects so that there would be a not too difficult path for someone to rise to a position of influence through diligence and intelligent decisions.

How to do it? Here again I do not have a ready solution.

One possibility is to introduce some negative feedback into the system of representation/delegation that would weaken the voting power for those who have a lot of it. This is an extremely tricky question that menaces to turn against the principle of proportionality so we should handle it with utmost care.

Populism – the Danger

The big danger of populism is that a crowd of individuals (whose intelligence and cognitive abilities lay everywhere on the Gaussian curve) are easily manipulated en-masse or self-manipulated through irrational movements of mind both leading to unreasonable modes of behavior.

This is a danger that we have to consider very seriously when contemplating any flavor of direct democracy. In case of this proposal the first countermeasure against the pitfalls of populism is the Second Criterion (vote proportional to contribution) which will work differently than the common crowd.

Behavioral studies show that if the crowd is divided into groups of 50-200 people who discuss issues together and communicate externally through a single representation the resulting behavior tends to be much more reasonable. Therefore the ideal configuration would seem to be that there are delegates representing 50-200 voters each. On the other hand it seems attractive to give every individual voter the option to exercise their own vote on the global level.

A good solution IMHO would make it possible for everyone to vote on their own but provide some powerful incentives for those representing the right amount of voters. (Financial and marketing support could do the job?) These representatives would probably be something we would call the upper middle class in economic terms – exactly the dignified respected grounded people who tend to be crucial for the stability of societies.

There would probably also appear an upper echelon of superstar representatives (probably 2nd and 3rd order representatives of representatives) speaking for millions of voters. While these may play an important role I do not see much need for them from the systems viewpoint.

Directionality – Who Controls Whom

The totalitarian governments have been very keen in abusing technology to control people – both their own citizens and those in other countries. Russian disinformation is the usual example and also there are disturbing news coming from China about the buildup of their digital surveillance state:

China invents the digital totalitarian state

Hello, Big Brother: How China controls its citizens through social media

These attempts are about government collecting data about the people and based on the collected data exerting power over those people.

In my opinion the powers of good must be equally aggressive in the opposite direction: Giving the people access to data about the governments and building digital channels for people to exert their power over the governments.

Subsidiarity – Deciding the Levels

The widely respected principle of subsidiarity seems simple: Issues should be decided on the lowest level of management on which they can be effectively handled. So far so good. However the arguments start when determining that lowest effective level of management.

This applies in terms of geography and specialization.

I would like to see some form of continual decision-making aimed at determining which decision belongs to which level of hierarchy.

I do not have such a model ready at the moment. I believe it should be a part of the prioritization voting which prepares motions to be voted on. So a motion could not only be prepared for voting but also moved to a lower (or higher) level of governance.

Complexity

It can be argued successfully that the expected complexity of global projects is beyond reasonable possibility and would lead to risks of extreme vulnerability and chaos. On the other hand there clearly do exist global challenges which can be addressed only on a global scale.

How can we design against the menace of overwhelming complexity?

- By keeping the rules and principles simple, straightforward and unambiguous
- By offloading complexity onto lower levels of the system e.g. localities and specialities. (Consistent with the established principle of Subsidiarity)

This design incorporates all the above opportunities to reduce the system complexity and thus mitigate the associated risks.

Keeping rules and principles simple

This is an omnipresent wisdom of programmers and system designers. Every small addition in complexity adds to the measure of possible chaos and difficulty in maintaining order and function. Another similar programmers' meme: "Design the data well and the program will write itself."

So the resulting attitude is to keep the designs as simple as possible as long as required functionality is achieved.

This is a principle similar to "Occam's razor" in scientific research which says that out of multiple explanations the simplest one is likely to be true.

Offloading complexity onto lower levels of the system

Systems are composed of multiple levels of functionality. Some of them are "core" essential existential functions, others may be less critical. It is almost an art form to define and separate these correctly.

Take for example a big email system like Gmail: In the core there sits an enormous engine which fulfills the simple function of transporting messages among its users not caring about their content, formatting, user comfort etc. It just passes and stores messages and must do so with extreme effectiveness and robustness.

On another level the user needs a comfortable "interface" to work with the email to handle sorting, formatting, automatic replies, spellchecking etc. etc. which are important but not critical. These are handled by separate subsystems, even from other vendors than the core. That is where some complexity may be offloaded without compromising the effectiveness of the core and of the whole.

Quantity of Laws

> *The more corrupt the state, the more numerous the laws.*
> *(Tacitus)*

The numbers and extent of laws in validity and those being produced is one very good measure of complexity of a political system. In the current democracies the parliaments tend to be extremely productive in issuing high numbers of laws beyond the comprehension of any individual thus increasing the complexities of their systems and opportunities for chaos.

I believe there should be limits to these numbers in a reasonable system. Limiting the voting to one new global law per week would seem like a reasonable level stemming from the idea that within one week a diligent person may be able to study a new problem and find at least some elementary orientation in a new topic before they vote on it.

This would also contribute toward keeping the global governance general and lean and focused on the really important and common issues while leaving many details to the diversity of regional and specialized bodies.

Obsolete Assumptions

The existing systems of governance from corporations to governments are based on some very antique preconceptions:

- a group of people has to gather in one place in order to communicate effectively and/or to make collective decisions
- a group of people numbering more than several hundred is too large to communicate and decide effectively => (so it has to make its decisions through a representative sub-group)
- since real time communication and sharing of information is impossible (=> it is impossible to oversee activities of the representing sub-group) the representation has to be selected for a fixed duration of time and left on their own for the duration of that time.
  - not to be mistaken for the healthy concept of "black box" encapsulation where – in order to reduce the complexity of transactions – we limit our attention to a defined set of inputs and outputs of a subsystem
- in group decision-making it is best to maintain the rule of one person – one vote to avoid cumbersome calculations

The new abilities attained by us – the Society – include:

- ability to effectively communicate in a group without gathering in one location
- ability to communicate in Real Time
- ability to include most or all population in real-time, all-geography communication
- ability to calculate decisions based on unwhole (fractional) numbers (*sometimes referred to as rational numbers :-)*)

These are the basic starting points from which we launch our design of the Governance Model

- Every person should be able to exercise a measurable bit of influence on the whole.
- Every person's input should be carried through the governance system in a way as direct as possible similar to a direct proportionality.
- Not every person has the will or capacity to worry about every decision. There delegation or representation comes  in which also serves for entrusting the decisions to someone plausible. These trustworthy representatives bring into the system their wisdom and ability to interpret and re-frame the questions and issues.

  The previous concept of representation is similar to the „Liquid Democracy" project.

- It is a reasonable goal to encourage direct voting by those who know what they are doing while the others should be represented.
- Technology can make our processes very fast but human beings need some time to think before making decisions.
- Some people and organizations are more powerful than others and the most usual measure of that power is finance. There is no use denying that power, rather it makes sense to acknowledge it and cooperate with it.
- Various juridical persons like states and corporations do exist and are important. They represent and serve people in various ways. Though they should not be granted any rights reserved for humans they should be included in the governance of common things.

- People are moved not by thoughts and concepts but by symbols, stories and personalities. Therefore apart from building a perfectly just voting machine there also is a need for symbols that one can identify with.

Design Decisions

A decision starts as a Motion submitted by anyone. It is prioritized in a queue in a continual vote by all the voters. If the Motion has been prioritized to the top of the queue it is elevated to be voted. The vote then decides whether the Motion is rejected or approved. If approved by the vote the Motion becomes a Decision. (Other decision paths e.g. a Continual Vote follow a similar philosophy.)

A single voting process evaluated by 2 criteria:
- One vote per physical person
- One vote per dollar contributed

In order for the vote to pass there has to be at least _50%_ consensus in both criteria. In other words a vote has to be agreed on by the majority of people and majority of contributors simultaneously.

Voters are both physical persons and juridical persons while only physical persons are entitled in the First Criterion / one vote per physical person. Juridical persons are entitled to voting power according to the Second Criterion – proportional to their contributions.

Credit Based Fluid Voting

After careful consideration I would not incorporate in the design any scheme where the voter could concentrate their voting power on certain issues while giving up on other, e.g. "Quadratic Voting". These may be worthwhile directions for later thought.

Representation

Any voter can vote personally or be represented by someone they trust. To be represented the voter gives their trust to a "Representative" meaning that the Representative is entitled and expected to vote on behalf of the voter in all votes. Changing Representatives should be freely allowed but not too frequently. When the voter has entrusted their voting power to a Representative they should still be able to vote personally on specific votes of their choosing.

Every person must select their representative even if they intend to often vote personally. If the person has not appointed a valid Representative a standard mechanism will get them one.

By default (meaning until a different decision is made) every voter is represented by their country government in order to bring the countries into the process.

Extremely powerful Representatives should be limited in their voting power to prevent monopolization of the voting process (*I do realize that this is a mortal sin against the principle of proportionality – however I see it as a measure against a greater un-proportionality such as the monopolization of the voting process.*)

Children

Children are human beings with all the corresponding inherent rights.
It has been an established principle that children do not have the abilities to decide for themselves, express their opinions and therefore cannot vote in democracies. There was little thought about this possibly stealing a part of their rights as humans. However having formulated the principle of Representation can open the discussion about how the children's rights could be implemented in a good system.

It would seem reasonable for a child to have the right to vote according to the 1st criterion while being represented by their parents. After reaching adulthood the new adult would be able to assign a different representative or vote directly. We might even see some adults leaving their representation assigned to their parents in a noble gesture of respect.

Assigning voting power to children would seem like an honest future-aiming philosophy: Those who raise children tend to care about the future *(their children's or their own)* so they should have more say in influencing the future.

Elections

Mathematically an election is a process of collectively selecting N winners from M candidates.

By candidates we usually mean persons but in a more general view we might be electing from a number of variants of some proposal. In this text let us speak about the election of persons.

In election the task is to pick a person from multiple candidates on whom the majority agrees. In elections run by a single criterion the task is quite simple: The one who gets the most votes wins. However when voting with two or more criteria of vote weights it gets a little more complicated: How do we calculate the final deciding (scalar) value when the votes are a vector of two components? Mathematically the task is to compute the length of the vector.

I can imagine several possibilities:

- Sum of the two components

- An arithmetic function similar to the Pythagorean theorem where the result of the pseudo-addition is greater than any one of the components but smaller than the sum of the components.

- The larger of the two components

- The smaller of the two components

The last option (The smaller of the two components) is my personal favorite. It is a simple principle and it says that the candidate needs to satisfy both criteria - if they excel in just one criterion it does not count without the other.

Electronic Voting

Voting electronically via secure telecommunications is the only realistic way of participatory global decision making. The electronic methods of voting, vote evaluation and accountability are being tested and used regularly.

There is an immense number of electronic voting systems and platforms being developed and tested like those listed here:

They are not without risks and many bad guys are eager to exploit any weakness found. Therefore the methods used must be carefully scrutinized on a continual basis in order to maintain a lead before the potential abusers.

Diversity of Tools

Some of the complexity of designing and running a huge global voting systems can be offloaded onto multiple subsystems (e.g. software components like user interface programs – probably created by independent parties) adhering to the same core principles but realizing them in various creative ways corresponding to different views and user priorities. Healthy diversity is one way to overcome the risks of excessive centralization.

Security

When using electronic communications and data processing security is of paramount importance. It will be a crucial factor in the implementation. When speaking of security one must be specific about the risks to be secure from. Some of them are

- Fraudulent or erroneous counting of votes
- Loss or theft of personal data

A system of global magnitude will be extremely attractive for misuse. It is often considered nearly impossible to achieve an excellent level of security in large systems. However an excellent level of security and trustworthiness is a necessary precondition, even more important than functionality itself.

While precise elaboration of security measures is beyond the scope of this document some of the measures would include:

- Testing the software and methodologies first in small scale e.g. in local communities
- Dividing the global system into parts using different technological solutions to achieve the same goals so that no single weakness would be common for the whole system
- Multiple redundant computing where the same task is achieved by several different methods and their results are compared for equivalence
- Using technological components already developed for very demanding applications e.g. banking or military
- ... etc.

Unlike in the next chapter where we will discuss components where technological functionality is prevalent here I would like to elaborate a kind of "components" where human reasoning prevails above technology – we might call them "Institutions":

Global Council

Let us propose the formation of a Global Council which is a virtual body of all voters around the globe who can vote on all common issues and have a certainty that their vote has been correctly counted. *(Therefore you and I and everyone else on Earth would become a member of this governing body with very small proportion of influence on the whole.)* The votes are weighted according to two criteria – number of people and amount of money contributed. For a "yes" vote there must be a *majority* in both criteria.

A physical representation of the Council is a gathering of the most influential ("weighted") representatives of voters in one place.

Presidium of the Global Council

is elected by the Global Council and serves to organize the decision-making processes of the Global Council. Presidium consists of 7 members elected in a specialized continual vote.

The role of the Presidium is to organize the work and voting of the Global Council, not to make decisions. For this purpose the members of the Presidium have special rights including the right to elevate proposals to a Voting status.

President

President is the Presidium Member who has received the most votes when the Presidency was vacant for reelection. The

President represents the Global Council and has special rights to elevate proposals to a Voting status.

Court of Procedure

Is an institution which guards that the voting of the Global Council has adhered to applicable rules and procedures. This is a key component which decides whether a voted Decision is compatible with applicable rules or whether for some reason it is invalid.

Its role is to stop a Motion or Decision if it

- was arrived at by incorrect procedure
- contains internal contradiction (a.k.a. Does not make sense)
- is impossible to execute

The court must be designed in a very conservative manner to provide needed stability and extreme responsibility of decisions.

Components of the Global Governance System

In this chapter I would like to discuss important components of technological nature. However apart from their technological functioning these components will also integrate a lot of human oversight and such they will be important institutions in their own right.

Identity Management System

The purpose of an Identity Management System (IMS) behind the governance model is to ascertain the identity of every individual – physical or juridical person – who interacts with the Governance System. The well thought-through design of this component will decide much of the whole system's resilience to various forms of potential fraud.

The function of IMS is to accept inputs from various sources formal and informal about individual identities and combine them into one worldwide list. The sources include formal and definitive ones like national registries and less official ones likes bank information or social media.

IMS (through machine protocols) will provide conclusive answers to the following standard questions:

- Is the person trying to access a system the one they are claiming to be?
  - If information provided by the accessing person is inadequate (e.g. a lost password) can we reach a certainty about their identity and act on it?
- Who is the person trying to enlist in the system – based on their national and other credentials?
- What voting weights are associated with a person?

While the technology behind the system is ready and proven the methodologies of evaluating numerous identity sources will be a challenging series of tasks requiring a large dedicated workforce.

Collateral Benefits of IMS

A Global IMS when created will be a unique tool for numerous commercial, governmental and societal application. For example it might well help social media in eliminating false persons sourcing fake news. As such the IMS may even pay for itself through commercial usage.

The IMS must be designed in accordance with the strictest rules on protection of personal data like the European GDPR.

Voting System

The Core Voting Functionality

The task here is to collect votes from billions of voters in the timescale of hours in such a way that each vote is accounted for. The computerized process seems to be a fairly simple one which is good for its robustness and reliability. Challenges will arise not from complexity but from the size of the task.

Scale

To assess the magnitude of the project one might begin by looking at the amount of data to be processed and stored in the course of one vote:

For an electorate of 10 billion (*we physicists calculate in orders of magnitude so don't want anything more precise from me*) the information would be on the order of $10^{13} - 10^{14}$ Bytes e.g. 10-100 TeraBytes. That amount would fit on 1-10 hard drives currently available on Amazon so this is no big deal. *I have personally managed a digital archiving project with storage of several PetaBytes e.g. at least 10 times larger than these requirements.* So in terms of data volumes we are firmly within the limits of current technology.

Another viewpoint is that the archive in my project took several years to fill while here we are in the timescale of hours.

In order to just transmit the desired volume of data within several hours we would be needing a throughput of 100 Gbps (Gigabits per second) or more. Nowadays we are installing networks of 1 Gbps throughput in our households so the desired capacity is not small but feasible in global dimensions.

Transmitting the data is one thing, processing them is another. Each byte of data has to go through transactions including cryptography and database operations. To estimate the requirements on computer power is very much guesswork. Very roughly we might compare such transactions to those of other giant online platforms, e.g. Google. It is estimated that Google process data on the order of 1 Petabit per second and growing. So it seems well within humankind's capability to process the voting data if we are willing to build something a little smaller (let's say one tenth) than Google.

User Access – a Variety

The basic principles and functioning of a global governance (a.k.a. voting) system can be defined in a very rational way. However the "User Interface" - e.g. the computer programming, graphics, etc. depend very much on users' subjective cognition and priorities and may vary across cultures. Like in many known cases this leads to separation between the core functionality of the system and its user interfaces.

This is not a new invention: For example a new EU directive on payment services (PSD2) will rule for all banks to offer their clients an electronic communication through a standard machine

interface. In plain language all the banks use the same „forms"
with the same fields on the internet. A piece of software on the
side of the client will then transform these plain fields into
something more appealing to the user.

The connection between a user interface and a computer system
is usually called API (Application Programming Interface) in
computer terminology. Through such an API the Global
Governance voting machine will manage its communication with
the global electorate.

It is usual that the provider of the core system also provides
some rudimentary user interface – as a backup if all else fails and
as a reference for various tests and examinations. This is a good
practice that I would recommend to follow.

The Third Party Interfaces will take many forms – desktop
computer programs, mobile applications, web services, maybe
even exotic interfaces like telephone answering automatons or
special fixtures for the handicapped. We can even imagine
existing providers adding a "Global Voting" function to their
pieces of software.   In other words the Third Party Interfaces
will enable immense creativity on the side of voter comfort and
support while observing all common rules and procedures built
into the core Global Governance voting system.

Discussions on Votable Topics

The previous thoughts about delegating parts of functionality to
independent software providers applies even more to the
provisioning of discussions about the voting.

Voting is the formal culmination of a decision-making process. It
is the tip of the iceberg whose major invisible part is a maze of
discussions among stakeholders offline and online, private and
public. Discussions are an essential part of any implementation
of a decision-making process.

Unlike the voting process the online discussions about a votable topic do not need to be strictly formal and structured. However they can make use of some data connected to the voting system

- Identity Management System can serve not only for voting but for many less formal functions as well including discussions. A discussion system can access information about who is a voter and/or how big voting power they represent etc.
- Voting proposals: Since the proposals which will later turn into votes are the important topics it seems natural that online discussions will spin around them. Therefore their incorporation into discussion system(s) seems like natural thing to do.

Since the functions to support public discussions do not need to be very formal they can well be handled by independent parties a.k.a. Servers – and not just one but many. I can easily imagine the voting proposals be discussed on Facebook and Twitter and Google Groups and many other servers all importing some common information and in diversity competing about who provides the best platform and the best discussion results.

Transaction Verification System

(TVS) In data processing systems a "Transaction" is anything that changes the input or output or internal state of a system. In this design a Transaction is the act of voting by a person. To make the system extremely trustworthy it must provide to every voter an unmodifiable record of how they voted and how their vote had contributed to the whole voting decision. This is not uncharted territory. We can take much inspiration from currently popular distributed cryptographic systems like the Blockchain that runs behind the famous digital currencies e.g. BitCoin. While the BlockChain itself will not be scalable to a global level some of its principles can be used. Actually the BlockChain is limited by its principle to include no single central node. Our task is simpler: We can afford to have a central node (or multiple cooperating nodes) for transactions as long as their outputs are distributed and archived in unmodifiable and trustworthy manner. This enables us a qualified assessment that the global system is feasible using current proven technologies.

The function of the "Transaction Verification System" (TVS) is to provide anyone with an answer to the question:

- How has the voter (with anonymized ID) X voted on issue Y and
- how has their vote contributed to the whole?

If each voter (knowing their anonymized ID) checks their past votes ex post then a certainty is achieved that all the votes were summarized correctly. The ex post checking does not have to rely on users' individual diligence – it can well be handled automatically by a multitude of third party programs that work with the voting system through machine protocols and make the process comfortable for the user.

In efforts to enable trustworthy verification of voting processes we might go even further: It would make a good sense to establish very powerful institutionalized overseers to make sure that all has worked right. *E.g. one might think of an office of "Guardian of the Checksum" or similar funny sounding titles.*

The following text is a quasi-legal expression of how the governance model should work. It tends to be unambiguous like a definition or a regulation but human-readable simultaneously.

Apart from the following technical rules there must be top-level "Constitutional" rules defining the fundamentals beginning with Human Rights. To change these top rules a higher level of consensus is required than for ordinary decisions. This is however beyond the scope of this document to elaborate.

Voters

A Voter is a natural or juridical person from anywhere on Earth whose identity is known and registered. To every voter two values are assigned:

- **First Criterion** value which equals 1 for every natural person and 0 for a juridical person
- **Second Criterion** value which equals 1 for every dollar contributed by the voter *in the past year* to common causes.

The Global Council is the collection of all voters.

Representation

A Voter may delegate their voting rights to another voter – a Representative. The Representative must not reward the voter for the delegation. The delegation is valid unless the voter chooses to vote explicitly on a particular Motion.

A State (a juridical person by definition) is by default the Representative of all its citizens under the condition that the citizens are

- free to select other Representative or vote independently and

- receive education and means to enable them to execute their individual voting rights in a qualified mode

A voter delegates to their selected Representative their voting powers based on both First and Second criteria inseparably.

The requirement for the people to receive education (not just about the voting system) could not be emphasized enough as it is the foundation of a reasonably behaving society.

Limitations of Representative Voting Powers

In order to prevent any one or group of voters from attaining an overwhelming power the following limitations apply:

- The weights according to the First Criterion of the highest 9 representatives are reduced to the value of the 10th representative.
- The weights according to the Second Criterion of the highest 39 representatives are reduced to the value of the 40th representative.

Motions

A Motion may be introduced by anyone (any Recognized Identity) into a Global Queue. A Continual Voting determines the priority in the queue.

The most prioritized Motions are regularly elevated for voting.

The Global President and members of Global Presidium have additional rights to elevate Motions for voting.

Voting

Voting Phase starts when a Motion is elevated to a voting status and ends one week later unless special provisions are used to shorten the period.

Voting is executed via secure telecommunications. A voter specifies whether they approve the Motion by an answer of Yes or No. The vote is anonymous.

A voter may change their vote and/or their Representative at any time during the voting period. The decisive value is the one valid at the end of the voting period.

Every voter (including Representatives) before voting on a Motion must prove that they are human and that they understand the question along with its consequences. This is realized in a brief test. The test must not give preference to any particular voting variant.

Votes are summarized in a way which provides

For all:

- Total sum of votes and their sum weighted according to First and Second criterion
- Auxiliary information enabling verification of the voting down to the level of each individual vote while respecting the voters' privacy

For each individual voter

- Chain of representations leading from the individual voter to the voting mechanism
- Their resulting vote as it resulted in the chain of representations

The total sum is calculated continually during the Voting Phase and is publicly available.

During the Voting Phase discussions are organized in both physical and virtual space. Active participation is prioritized according to the voting power represented by the participant.

Decisions

A Decision is made based on a Motion which has received more than 50% of executed votes in the First Criterion (one vote per person) and simultaneously more than 50% of executed votes in the Second Criterion (one vote per dollar contributed).

After the vote a Decision enters an Examination Phase of *4 weeks* duration in which it may be annulled by

- Vote of *60%* or more in the First or Second Criterion at any time during the Examination Period

- Ruling of the Court of Procedure at any time during the Examination Period

The Examination Phase may be shortened using special provisions to facilitate emergency decisions.

Continual Voting

Continual voting serves to provide an uninterrupted timely answer to constant questions, namely

- Election of individuals to certain roles
- Prioritization of Motions for voting
- Budget allocations

The voters may apply their votes or change them at any time even when currently the vote has no immediate effect.

Continual Voting to Elect Presidium

A voter answers the question "Whom do I want to be a member of Presidium?" The voter can divide the weight of their vote among any number of candidates.

Every Presidium Member including the President has their seat guaranteed for *1 year* from the moment of election.

The president additionally remains Presidium Member for *1 year* after the end of their presidency. A seat becomes free for a reelection after a Presidium Member no longer has their seat guaranteed.

If no seat is currently vacant then the Continual Election has no immediate effect – it provides only an informational feedback. Once a seat is free for reelection the continual vote comes into effect to fill that seat.

Role of the Existing States

The current (mostly national) states do exist and have to be respected. They can very well be used in their primary function of ascertaining the identity of their citizens for the purpose of authentication. *(For example we would likely trust even an ID card from North Korea in lack of better identification.)*

The idea is that the existing national states will be pulled in to represent their citizens in voting and to contribute funds. The states should be motivated to participate by a desire to execute their power of default representation of their citizens in global voting.

OK, so we have a wonderful plan. Now let us examine whether and why should people and institutions accept it and support it, even submit to it.

Why Should They Come on Board

Some may favor a new model of governance because they expect it to be good for the society. However it seems realistic that most will evaluate the offer from selfish viewpoints. Therefore if a majority of selfish interests could be satisfied then the plan could be successful.

Rich People

The really rich people hoard more money not to buy more things but to buy more power. This is well discussed in an <u>article "Six Things We Can Learn About US Plutocracy By Looking At Jeff Bezos"</u>

This plan is a clean offer of power for money, legal and regulated.

However it can be often seen that the rich seek not just power for its own sake but also engage in various charities either to do good or to boost their egos. The Proportional Governance model can give them an opportunity to do both. With the provision of Departmental Recursion one could even decide toward which actions to direct the power of their money (and get a say in that field). I can well imagine the likes of Jeff Bezos contributing toward (and co-deciding about) space exploration and Bill Gates maybe toward global healthcare.

Actually it is the rich visionaries who could get a Global Council started even before any of the nations or massive middle class people embrace it.

Corporations

should be interested because of the simple fact that this mechanism would give them an official say in public matters for the first time.

Rich Countries

The developed countries, being major contributors to international charities and activities like the U.N. should want to get a more proportional share of decision-making influence in these activities.

Poor Countries

Poor and especially overpopulated poor countries should wish to leverage the quantity of their citizens – eligible voters. The requirement for these voters to become educated to well exercise their voting rights would naturally attract help from global sources toward education and informing in those countries.

Danger of Militant Organizations

It must be taken into account that the presented system could be abused by well disciplined groups like some dictatorial militant movements. The danger is that the individual voting power of the controlled people might be bent to represent the dictators which would be quite counterproductive.

One thing is imagining and designing a wonderful concept or a system. Another very different thing is implementing it successfully.

It is inevitable that plenty of talented bad guys will invest great effort into abusing any weaknesses or flaws in the system. Therefore it would make sense to develop, test and implement gradually, from small scale to large, so that errors can be treated along the way.

Step 0: Prepare Support

This is actually the first prerequisite before starting anything practical. It is necessary to get enough financial and publicity power behind the plan.

As or the initial finance it can acquired from a grassroots movement perhaps through one of the crowdfunding platforms and/or from several rich visionary supporters. A similar kind of people have the power to provide the publicity needed to get a mass following.

It is my hope that one of the existing groups including the Global Challenges Foundation will be successful at this task and use its influence to launch a reform similar to the one proposed here.

Step 1: Develop Tools

Software and Systems

It is clear that the presented Governance Model will need to be supported by special software along with its implementation methodologies. These components can be developed in advance before any critical global decisions are made and can even go a long way toward proving their worth.

One thing is developing the software with global scalability in mind and another thing is implementing that software as core of a global governance system. Both are difficult tasks but the first one can be done in advance in a safe environment though not without expenses.

My preliminary estimate of the cost of development of globally scalable voting software and associated protocols is in the order of ten million USD while the global scale implementation is expected to cost about one order of magnitude more. These are very rough numbers intended just to assess the magnitude of the problem and will have to be followed by real precise budgets.

Identity Management

The component most ready for immediate deployment regardless of political decisions is the Global Identity Management System (IMS).

The trick here that a single IMS would serve numerous implementations of voting systems possibly varying widely in their methodologies and rules. In spite of their differences they will all need to pinpoint the identities of every person in the global realm and this is where the unifying magic of the IMS comes to the rescue.

Develop Strategy and Methodology

Along with technology and software comes the need to know how to handle those technologies. It is well known that technologies installed without sufficient effort on „implementation" (e.g. making it fit the current context of organizational structures and human activities in its vicinity) have often failed precisely because of that inadequacy.

There exist well developed proven methodologies of controlling various implementation processes so we would not be inventing anything new.

The idea here is that ways of implementing the decision-making system(s) must be pre-planned, recorded, judged in hindsight and made available for others to follow.

Step 2: Establish Symbols

People are moved by images and stories, not by concepts. Therefore it is crucial to well design the symbolic images for people to identify with.

Images and Sensorics

Please start with proposing your own version of global symbols: A flag, a logo/emblem, anthem…

At this point I - *like most creative guys* - would be tempted to immediately propose my own idea of a Global Flag and give my proposal a head start. That would be wrong because a good symbol must come from a collective debate so that people could identify with the symbol.

As a negative example I would name one excellent and smart proponent of a Mars mission who one day came and said "This IS the flag of Mars" showing something so ugly (in my own subjective opinion – sorry I do have opinions and am subjective) that it immediately raised unpronounced questions like "Do I really want to rally behind THIS flag?" even though the ideas and concepts were very good ones. Such a seeming triviality can have significant effect on people's support or lack thereof so let us be very careful and considerate here.

If a common symbol is arrived at through some agreeable process it is more acceptable even by people who do not agree with the decision.

The best symbols are the ones that arise from grassroots spontaneously.

Places

Do we need a special place to make a concept appear real? Maybe we do. Anyway we need places to house administrative staff necessary for any management or governance and to facilitate physical meetings of stakeholders (Meeting physically in all the richness of a personal encounter still has some advantages over interacting in cyberspace.) So we may need some version of a capital city or cities.

I would prefer to avoid the image of a majestic center of imperial power such as Rome or the never realized Germania or maybe even Washington D.C. or Moscow. Rather I would like to see places of work and encounters situated at remarkable geographies around the world. The spirit of the place (*genius loci*) - natural or cultural – should always surpass the self-importance of the contained managerial structures.

Just imagine a conference center located under Mount Everest – or next to the Stonehenge – what a powerful message would that location convey to its attendees regarding the relationship of humankind to nature and Cosmos and to our own heritage.

In my humble opinion there should be multiple centers of global management, not a single imperial megalopolis.

And I see no reason why the location of capital places should have to be permanent. Instead there are good reasons for periodically moving of institutions among places. A change of location and housing tends to bring refreshing consequences into the inside of managerial structures. A move every 20 years would seem like a good natural cycle.

(As the architects say "The house always wins" meaning that a building influences its inhabitants in myriads of subtle ways – for better or for worse. So designing and populating a new building may support innovation which is what we want right now. That does not exclude the possibility that a time may come when stability will become more valuable than innovation and places will become more permanent – but we are not there yet.)

People

The image of the King is a powerful archetypal concept. He impersonates all that his kingdom stands for and communicates his values naturally all around. Even in democracies and supposedly collective ✳cracies there tends to appear one leader who carries the public image of it all. A question is whether we need such a "global president" - a figure of powerful public image and identification. I am not sure. I would be much more comfortable with collective decision-making bodies, but

- *„No collective has ever written a symphony"* and
- A collective is much more difficult to identify with that a single personality

So it would seem that the Global Governance should likely be personified by the most obvious king figure – the President of the Global Council.

Rituals

Rituals have a huge power to convey deep messages and have them imprinted into people's minds and subconsciousness.

Well designed rituals can very expressly mark important moments in life of an individual or a society. Our current society has very much lost this understanding and is thus at a great loss. For an example take a look at the opening scenes of Yefremov's movie "Andromeda Nebula" (though the movie is naive by today's standards).

Even simple tasks like transferring a role from one person to another can attain a deep meaning when expressed by a smart ritual.

Just imagine the act of paying and receiving a salary. My salary just appears on my bank account and that is it. Would it not be much more powerful if my employer handed me the money and said "Thank you for your work" and I replied "Thank you for the pay." Powerful and dignified.

In my humble opinion a new form of governance should develop with it new effective rituals as well – and continue reinventing them before they fade into boredom.

Step 3: Start Small on the Bottom

We are speaking here about a disruptive innovation in the processes of collective decision-making a.k.a. Politics. The current methods have been growing for centuries and there is a lot of value and certitude in their continuity. It would be extremely foolish to even contemplate a sudden disruptive innovation that would put those certitudes at risk by experimenting with untested innovation.

Therefore the innovations should first be tested and proven in less critical contexts where the risks are small. These could be small municipal processes or organizations (big or small) where things are uncluttered and transparent enough to permit solid observation of how the new process works.

This includes an element of evolution as opposed to revolution: A new system of governance may prove successful at some levels and fail at other levels. So its implementation could still serve well in some situations even if it does not reach the omnipotent global scale. A gradual chain of implementations and practical real-life experiments is the process that would show where the limits are.

Organizations

There are numerous independent organizations that could profit from reasonable well structured proportional decision-making. There are no great barriers preventing an organization from adopting a software tool to organize its internal voting and decision-making. This may be the first proving ground for adoption of the new ways for many.

To make the adoption of the proportional governance as easy as possible for an organization there should be freely available software for the implementation along with publicly accessible methodologies and guides to help anyone who wants it.

Regional Politics

The next steps is to convince the people around the world about the validity of the effort and have the conviction expressed in elections inside the national states.

Since many political systems are based on political parties and this principle is enforced by laws it may be necessary to set up a dedicated „global" party in some countries to take part in elections. Elsewhere it may suffice to employ an existing party (which adapts itself to the global ideology) as a vehicle in the election process.

Given the duration of the election cycle in most countries this step should take about 6 years.

Engage in non-conflicting activities

In the beginning the Global Governance needs to establish its authority and deploy its structures. Before getting real political power it can start with global activities that produce the least conflict against the established status-quo. These may include:

- Education and culture,
    - Educating the populations about the governance itself in the context of open reasonable society. Great priority.
- Humanitarian efforts including disaster relief,
- Ecology including climate change,
- Technical standardization,
- Science and exploration including space exploration

International Organizations

Many international organizations could benefit from using a Proportional Governance model. Some of them might come forward in implementing it on an international or global scale. That would give model a necessary proving across multiple cultures and multiple geographies – inevitable for a truly global application.

Let us assume that the Proportional Governance model has been successfully implemented in organizations and has proven its worth. Then comes a time when it can take the biggest step – to connect all the levels from bottom to top through democratic changes.

The decisive moment is creating a public trust toward the model that trickles into the inside of political parties and enables a discussion about implementing the model on the scale of national governments through regional governing bodies (parliaments, governments) - as in step 3. Those governing bodies will then be ready to voluntarily integrate into a larger decision-making structure and hopefully to transfer some authority from the existing states to the Global.

This is the moment where greatest risk is waiting. There are countless examples of benevolent groups and individuals who came to political power with good intentions but could not cope with the immense demands on their integrity and organizational skills. This has often lead to corrupted decision-making and growth of unhealthy powers. One safe way of mitigating such an outcome would be to

- establish the formal authority in gradual steps to maintain control over the process
- have all the necessary structures prepared in advance to cushion the shock

Especially it is crucial for the decision-making processes e.g. voting to be in place and proven well before a formal authority is entrusted to them.

Along a similar line: Nothing could be more important that educating and preparing the right people for their new governance roles. Under any scenario the risks will be great and one could not be too prepared.

The term „easy step“ is getting especially sarcastic in this phase because this might be the most difficult and risky step humankind has ever taken. To make a radical change in power structures without violence would be perhaps THE greatest achievement.

Step 6 through ∞ : Change

Live happily ever after?

Not at all. All systems have a limited lifetime and have to be maintained and modified regularly to function well. This or any other system of global governance will have a finite lifetime and should include provisions to be reformed and eventually dismantled in favor of something new.

The proposed system includes many possibilities of its own reforming through timely changes of parameters. Through such careful design it might remain functional for a long time without having to be dismantled. If democracies could last for centuries we should be expecting and planning at least a similar timescale for any new system of public decision-making.

As an intellectual exercise regarding flexibility of the model let us think through this example:
Colonies will be established on the Moon and Mars. They will be literally off the Globe so how will „Global“ governance apply to them? How will the model be expanded to cover such a situation? Will the architecture be ready for it? Will the processes be efficient enough to make interplanetary rebellions pointless? And how about an interstellar colony where a signal (=vote) will take years to travel back and forth. Will the system be ready for that?

Linear Global Governance Model

The following text was submitted to "The Global Challenges Prize 2017: A New Shape – Remodelling Global Cooperation" Competition.

For rules and other information about the competition please refer to https://globalchallenges.org/en/our-work/the-new-shape-prize

The Original

The original submission along with clarifications is available at

http://governance.svobodat.com/GCFC_paper_SvobodaT.pdf

Earlier I had intended to include a full text of the original submission in this book. However it was viewed as confusing for the reader as some of the text would be duplicate. So I have decided to include only a link and illustrations.

Illustrations

Please note that the illustrations have used the older term "Linear" which has since been superseded by "Proportional".

Fig. 1 Voting Paths

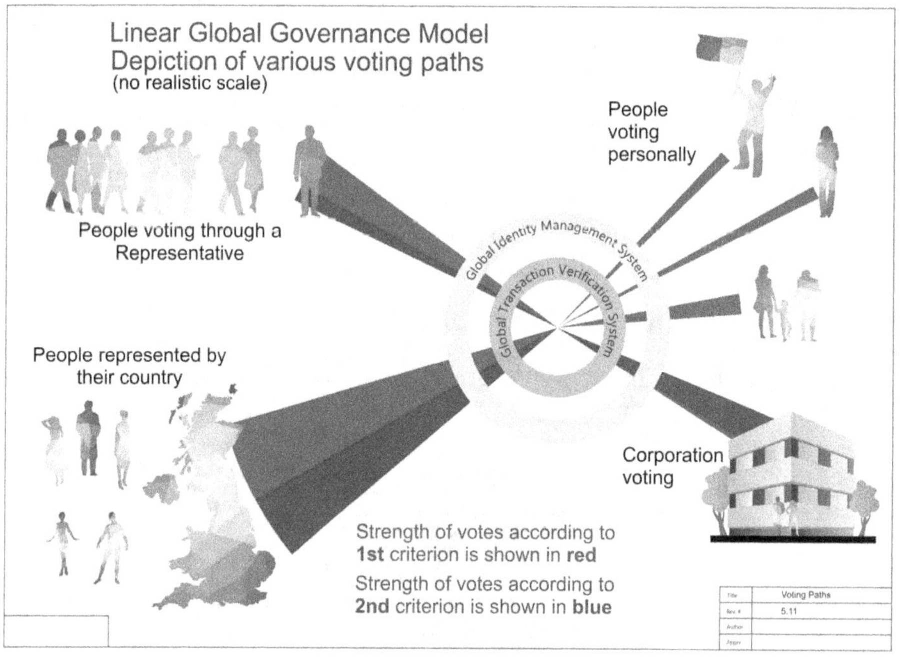

For a better view of the image see

http://governance.svobodat.com/Fig1_Voting_paths_v06.pdf

Fig. 2 Voting Process

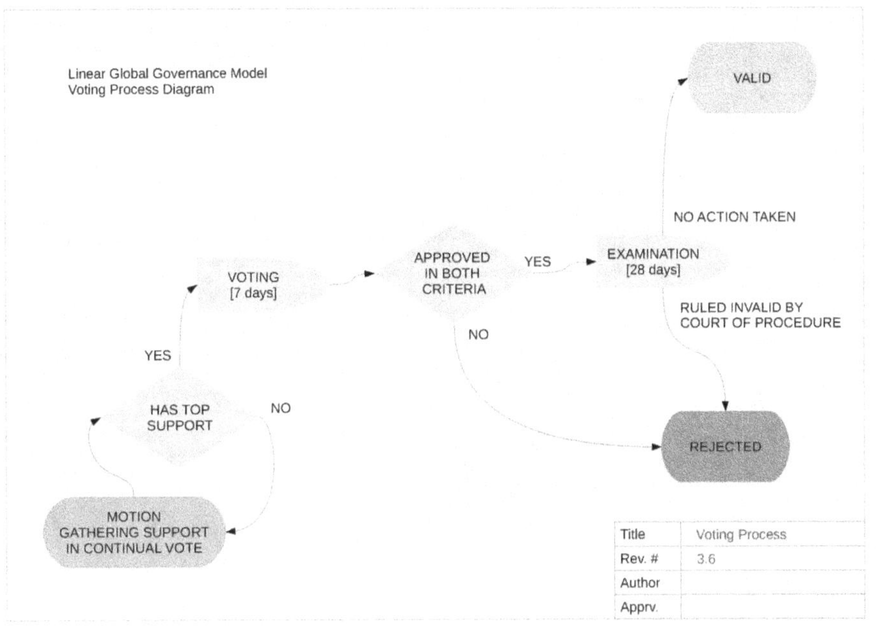

Title	Voting Process
Rev. #	3.6
Author	
Apprv.	

For a better view of the image
see http://governance.svobodat.com/Fig2_Voting_process_v04.pdf

Fig. 3 Voting Influences

This image did not make it to the submission because the limit was 2 illustrations.

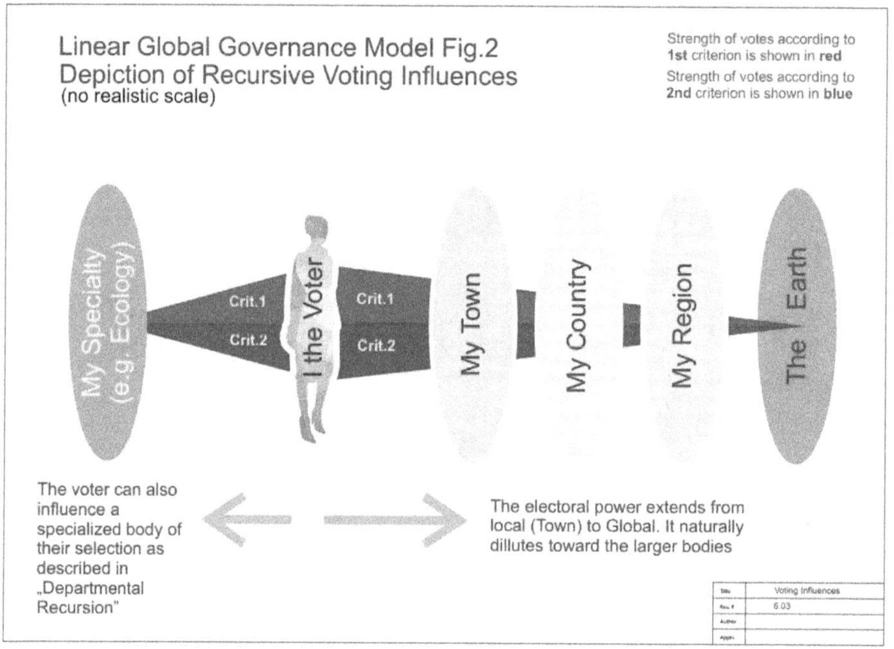

For a better view of the image see

http://governance.svobodat.com/Fig3_Voting_influences_v06b.pdf

Thank you so much for reading this book. I hope very much that there was something you liked about it.

If you have found this book of value you are cordially invited to connect to its community on Facebook

This book is available for download for free in order to better spread its message. However the time and resources needed to produce the book and its followups are not free so please consider helping the effort by purchasing the book or contributing by other means using this link

If you have already bought and this plea is coming to you through a paid copy then please accept my big thanks.

File: 6_Steps_089

Date: 2018-03-21